Look What I Found!

At the Seaside

Paul Humphrey

W
FRANKLIN WATTS
LONDON • SYDNEY

This edition 2009

Franklin Watts
338 Euston Road
London
NW1 3BH

Franklin Watts Australia
Level 17/207 Kent Street
Sydney
NSW 2000

© Franklin Watts 2005

Planning and production by Discovery Books Limited
Editor: Geoff Barker
Designer: Ian Winton
Natural history consultant: Michael Chinery
Language consultant: Helen Barden
Photographer: Chris Fairclough, including front cover

Additional photographs: Bruce Coleman: 16 (Kim Taylor),
17 (C.&S. Hood), 19 (Jane Burton); NHPA: 11 (Matt Bain),
21 (Laurie Campbell), 25 (Yves Lanceau).

A CIP catalogue record for this book is available from the
British Library

ISBN 978 0 7496 8914 8

Dewey decimal classification number: 577.69'9

Always go for a walk with an adult. Take care around water.

Printed in China

Franklin Watts is a division of Hachette Children's Books,
an Hachette UK Company.
www.hachette.co.uk

Lo
WI
I Fo

Contents

I went to the seaside and
this is what I found.
There were high cliffs
across the bay.

The beach had
yellow sand,
pebbles and grassy
sand dunes.

I wriggled my toes in the fine, warm sand.

I liked these flowers.

I followed these footprints in
the wet sand.

Lugworms had
made lots of little
sand squiggles.

**lugworm
cast**

lugworm

A dead starfish had been washed up on the beach.

A little crab quickly hid
under the sand.

I walked along the beach
to look at the rocks.

The rocks were slippery.
They were covered in
slimy seaweed and shells.

whelks

I peered into a rock pool.
I saw some tiny black
creatures moving about.

They were springtails.

Sea anemones waved their
tentacles around.

The seaweed was different colours.

I moved a piece with my toe ...

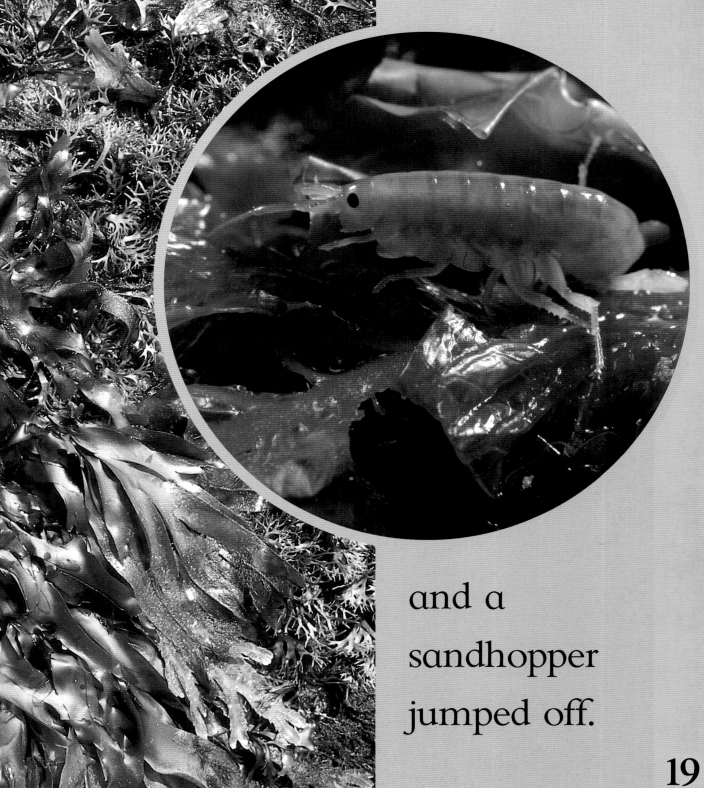

and a
sandhopper
jumped off.

I walked on and came to
a pebbly beach. I heard
the crash of waves.

The waves splashed back
and forwards, all frothy
and white.

I saw a wobbly jellyfish.

I picked up some pebbles.
Some had been worn
away by the waves.

They felt smooth in my hand.

I found some beautiful shells too.

I heard seagulls squawking.

They were
looking for
fish to eat.

One seagull perched near me.

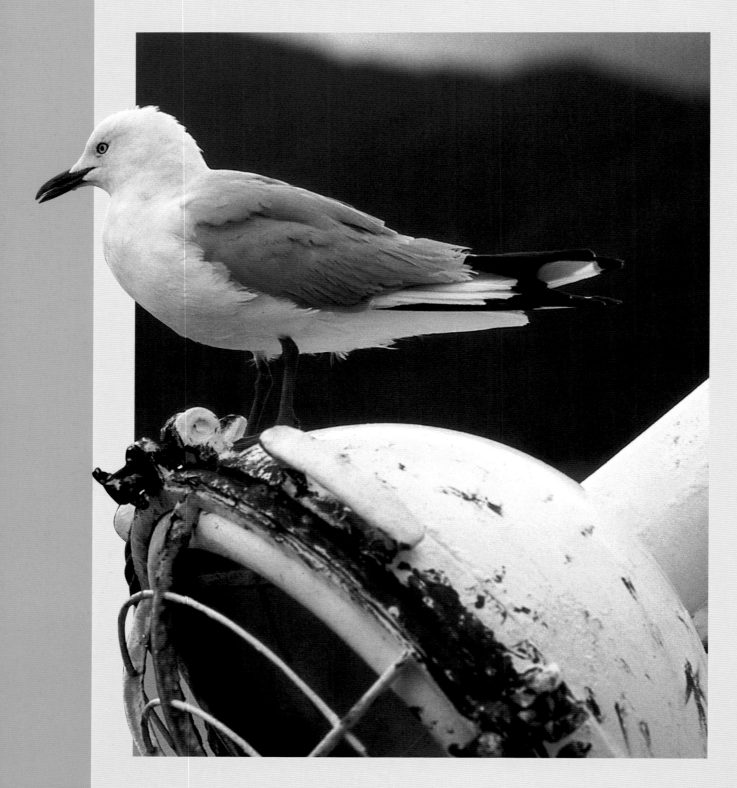

Waves crashed on the rocks.
The tide was coming in and
the sun was setting.

Time to go home.

Can you find these in the book?

flowers

whelks

starfish

seagulls

crab

seaweed

Index